Travelling Second Class

CW00662699

Poetry by Henry Normal

Is Love Science Fiction?

Love Like Hell

Does Inflation Affect the Emotion?

A More Intimate Fame

Do You Believe in Carpetworld?

The Dream Ticket

The Fifteenth of February

The Third Person

Nude Modelling for the Afterlife

A Map of Heaven

Staring Directly at the Eclipse

Travelling Second Class Through Hope

HENRY NORMAL

Flapjack Press
flapjackpress.co.uk

Exploring the synergy between performance and the page

Published in 2017 by Flapjack Press
Salford, Gtr Manchester
flapjackpress.co.uk

ISBN 978-0-9955012-6-3

Photographs courtesy of the author
Design by Brink

Printed by Imprint Digital
Upton Pyne, Exeter, Devon
imprintdigital.com

The poems in this collection previously appeared in:

Is Love Science Fiction?, *Love Like Hell*,
Does Inflation Affect the Emotion?, *A More Intimate Fame*,
Do You Believe in Carpetworld?, *The Dream Ticket*,
The Fifteenth of February, *The Third Person*
and *Nude Modelling for the Afterlife.*

Dedicated to my sister, Linda Hallam,
for a lifetime of support.

I'd like to thank Theresa Sowerby, Penny Shepherd and Paul Neads for their help in bringing this collection together.

Contents

From the first poem I defy you not to be transported into the very particular, unique and entrancing world of Henry Normal.

I had the good fortune to be transported some thirty years ago. It was through a series of tours, performances and publications. It was a time when comedians performed with poets who performed with songwriters: the packet of three in the Madchester maelstrom were Henry Normal, Johnny Dangerously and me. Johnny became John Bramwell of I am Kloot, I continued as a poet and Henry became one of the most successful British comedy producers of the 20th Century.

Back then if 'Madchester' had a poet laureate it would have been Henry Normal. To me, Normal was famous already. He was known across the UK as a hilarious and yet serious poet. And as the one who bridged the gap between rant/punk poetry and a new generation of 'performance poets'. Henry has little truck with these limiting terms, as do I.

His wit stands aside his melancholy, much like Spike Milligan, whose wit and melancholy can also devastate an audience. Like Milligan, Normal changed culture through his comedy, but never relented from his poetry. It is not that poetry took a back seat. It was the drive. It was the engine. In his most private most intimate most truthful moments on the red carpets amongst the flashing lights of paparazzi he told himself what I always knew, that he was first and foremost a poet.

I have never seen a busier poet than Henry Normal. He would drive to an event on the other side of the country and return the same night to write scripts for his friend, the relative newcomer, Steve Coogan. Their relationship would go on to become defining of a culture and era. After a couple of Radio 4 comedies and TV appearances Henry moved, wholesale, across to comedy.

Altruism is not a common trait in poets. But it's a central if hidden theme in the career of Henry Normal. It's little known that he is the originator and architect of The Manchester International Literature Festival. I can't help thinking that MILF is his own joke. It isn't. Please don't google MILF. Manchester International Literature Festival started in his imagination and then he made it happen. It is now a mainstay of the literary landscape of Britain. *MILF.*

And yet before all this, before even arriving in Manchester in the 1980s, and before he set up home in a one bedroom flat in the defiantly unhip Crumpsall, he'd already had his own record store in Chesterfield. He'd already been a punk poet supporting local combo Pulp. You could say that Jarvis Cocker (the lead singer of Pulp) is the musical mirror of Henry Normal the poet.

Adrian Mitchell said, "Most people ignore most poetry because most poetry ignores most people.". Although I question why poetry should be interested in *other* people I agree with the sentiment. The specific becomes universal in much the same way as Nan Shepherd feels about a mountain. I feel this in Henry's commitment to the poem and to poetry.

Put simply, Henry Normal is a genius. He is a genius of the spoken word and of the performed word and of the written word. I suggest you google him. Google is the new library. The canon will be decided via google more than through the libraries of Oxford or Cambridge. The canon will be crowd-sourced and quality will always win out.

We are fortunate to be "travelling second class through hope". I am fortunate that Normal has returned to his first love – poetry. Henry Normal. Poet. He lives with his wife and son. Their kitchen window looks out at the English Channel with its hourly tidal streams: a poet, his wife and their son on the tides of time once again gracing our shores.

In *Travelling Second Class Through Hope* we have many of my favourite poems from Henry's books. Become familiar with him, reacquaint yourself, as you would with a friend who has returned from his travels with the same smirk. He is wiser, funnier, stronger, and more appreciative that he is here with his loved ones. His poems. His family.

I count Normal amongst my favourite living poets: Benjamin Zephaniah, Kathleen Jamie, Caroline Bird, Kate Tempest, Linton Kwesi Johnson, Jackie Kay, John Agard, Grace Nichols... His rightful place amongst them is well deserved. Welcome home Henry Normal. The fire is on and the kettle is boiled. Now where are the biscuits: Garibaldi anyone?

Travelling Second Class
Through Hope

Embarrassed like the moon at midday

I set my watch 30 minutes fast this morning
and watched myself sleep a while

touching the edges of the universe
others existing only in dreams

I pulled back the curtains
and witnessed the world coping without me

All day
I caught the change in people as I entered their lives

Saw how differently they behaved before I arrived
It was as if I was watching them dressing

Tomorrow I'll set my watch back an hour to see how other edges
close in as I leave

See myself as ghost in other dreams

Sans pretension

We say 'cul-de-sac'
to make 'dead end' sound sunny
We say 'nouveau riche'
instead of working class with money

We call art 'avant-garde'
when we don't understand it
Jumble sales sell 'bric-à-brac'
which must be French for shit

Let's call a spud a spud
no more lies or elaborate word contortions
Chips are chips
not pommes frites or french fries
Why say 'haute cuisine' when you mean 'smaller portions'

No more saying we had a 'tête-à-tête'
when you mean you've been nagging
bragging or just chin wagging

And no more calling it a 'ménage à trois'
when you mean three people shagging

The first time I died I was completely hopeless at it

There's St Peter at the gates of Heaven
doesn't know whether to close early for lunch
or hurry me up

God's scratching his head
The Devil's re-checking his inventory

Yes... no...?
People dying about me right left and centre
not giving it a second thought

There's me – more trouble than I'm worth
Dithering
Stuck in some universal revolving door
waving my arms about, trying to attract attention

Am I early?
Er... Shall I come back later?
Er... Is there a queue? Er...

Some cherubim start to put down their harps
and come to see what all the fuss is about

Others play louder hoping I'll go away

Past relatives, realising it's me, skulk off
into a blinding light

The Devil starts looking concerned
and sneaks out a bottle of Tippex

Sitting on the idea of grass

Sitting on grass
worms writhe in wet soil only a breath beneath the surface
insects inch between blades

This is not the idea of grass
upon which you're sitting

of village cricket and croquet on the lawn
of parasols and summer picnics
of green carpets and rose gardens

Eating cheese
it is not the view through the microscope you are eating

Admiring a body
it is not the tissue and fibres, the bones and the organs you
hold in mind

Falling in love
you select your level of perception

Eternity comes and goes as easy as that
like the crossing of the equator
or the passing of infection
there is something, then there is nothing
and somewhere in-between
there is change

Blood rushes from the heart to the head
and back to the heart
once, twice
and somewhere on its return
or its migration out again
there is change

Breath enters the lungs and
is expelled
once, twice
and somewhere between the expulsion
and the intake of fresh air
there is change

Sensation excites the nerves
the pupils dilate and retract
pores react to temperature
yet even without perceived movement
time passes
there is change

Images illustrate the mind
some erratic, some fluid
conscious and subconscious
some casual, some revealing deliberation
the world outside is as yet unaltered but
there is change

65 million years BC – February 3rd – Thursday

To Hell with the lot of them, that's what I say.
This ice age is no place for a poet.
Fight and eat, eat and fight, that's all they know.
It's like talking to an amoeba.
'We need to evolve,' I told them.
'We need a thumb.'
'Warm blood,' I said. 'That's the future.'
But all they do is stomp around trying to look frightening.
Nothing much happening. Went to bed early.

65 million years BC – February 4th – Friday

'Ok let's invent fire,' I said.
No response.
'What about the wheel?'
Nothing.
We foraged around for leaves for a while.
Alan tried to charge a tree.
There was nothing we could do for him.

65 million years BC – February 5th – Saturday

A stegosaurus next to me in the mud is bleeding.
He's resting between bouts with a pterodactyl.
I explained to him about air superiority.
Suggested we improve our ground-to-air technology.
He tried to gouge me with his horn.
I've got a bad feeling we're not going to make it.

65 million years BC – February 6th – Sunday

There's fierce fighting near the ravine.
No-one seems to have noticed the ice is receding.

I don't like the look of the dust that's
blowing in from the south.
Everyone's moving out.
I showed the General my plans for an 'eco-dome'
which I believe could maintain and perpetuate a friendly
environment indefinitely.
He ate them.

65 million years BC – February 7th – Monday

This morning we came across a herd of creatures we had never
seen before. All of them were dead.
A couple of the older tyrannosaurs wanted to turn back.
Fires are burning all around us now.
It's hard to tell the difference between night and day.
I can't believe there is still fighting.
The only thing that pulls me through is I know in my heart
God is on our side.

65 million years BC – February 8th – Tuesday

I woke up sweating. No idea of the time.
I tried to find out as I have a feeling these little details
are important somehow.
Anyway the point is I'd been dreaming.
Well it was more of a nightmare really.
All I can remember was that I was dead,
and someone or something had re-assembled my bones
but had gotten it wrong.
I tried to correct them, diplomatically at first, but they
assured me they knew more about it than I did.
We began to fight. That's when I woke up.
I'm not sure of the time. It was late, I know that.

Lying about your age

Against nature you choose to stunt progression

Devaluing yourself
betraying new friends
you dishonour cherished moments
and demean suffering for mathematics

Instant time travel within a vacuum
you lose faith
misalign the stars
and redraw the truth as misfit

Never play chess with an anarcho-nihilist

I tried to play chess with an anarcho-nihilist once
Every move I made he questioned

He continually changed the rules
but later claimed that there weren't really any in the first place

He said 'Any piece can go to any position on the board it wants
when it wants'

He kept making three or four moves at a time
Then when it suited him he moved my pieces out of the way
Sometimes into other rooms

He refused to place any of the pieces centrally in the proper squares
He declared such divisions to be 'false borders'
and started painting out the white squares at random

When I announced it was check mate and that I'd won
he just kicked the table over and
flushed my king down the loo

It's always harder for the gardener
to smell how sweet the flowers are
with the stench of manure still on his palms

From the first warm blood in the water
nature has never invested in failure
A call for moral justice would have us all shot at dawn

There's more courage in the hand that re-enters the flame
than in all the arrogance of those yet to fail

Your room

You're painting your nails
in your bedsit coffin
cleaning your mug whilst still drinking your coffee

eating sleeping drinking and waiting
as the tears dry you're there repainting

cleaning up the dust the Hoover missed
never allowing anything to rust
nothing must, not in your room

You're changing the cover and matching pillows
painting out mirrors
and painting out windows in your room

Between brush strokes you're hesitating
I know you're in there
I can hear you painting

A baby magpie

Yet only a few days old
in moments of solitude that follow
does this life even now herald
a little sorrow

Concerning loss and theft

I've lost something valuable or had it stolen
So I'm forced to retrace my mundane actions
these tiny harbingers whose whispers
now mock with megaphones

The margin of error
I've recently allowed myself
widens from the gap at back of a settee
to the Grand Canyon

Re-assessing even the most casual of contact
my mistrust embitters charity
I've become Machiavelli dusting for prints
undermining all integrity in trial by memory

No matter whether it turns up
or not
I feel I've lost something valuable
or had it stolen

**There will come a time you will no longer set aside
one day a week for tears**

your heart seems hesitant between each beat
and serenity is never so easily charted
not even on the most detailed atlas

for there appears an honesty
within your quiet breathing
to which these sad poems aspire

it is time, perhaps
to set aside a little compassion
and to court yourself

Heavy Goods Vehicle

hugging
the
inside
lane

a giant
morse
code

we
own
the
dark
road
home

stamina
not
speed
now
virtue

a slow
cure
along
the
back
bone

sleep
walking
beyond
the
cathode

pilgrims
and
heroes

Stealing the scream

Poetry reduced to the metric
the shrill too raw for comfort, the anguish untidy
The pitch not conducive to the cosy aesthetic
Sport replaces anarchy

Concealed and congealed in the mud mundane
defined and refined in reason
The sum of mass and energy remains
yet something divine is missing

In a world without scrapes, Pluto remote
my shadow cast in outline only
I have been rendered sedate, the wrong ghost
there is no desperation to pierce me

Skeleton

My teeth are somewhat corroded by sugar
but otherwise despite my figure
my skeleton is not dissimilar to yours

My muscles are weak and wasted
and through lack of use have degenerated
but these will rot long before my bones

My stomach and my legs are swollen
my neck and jowls have become misshapen
All this will disappear as we grow nearer

The soothing of elasticity has deserted my face
my eyes have lost focus with age
soon my hair will begin to skulk away

There is a scent and a texture to my skin
that has at times been found attractive
This will quickly lose its lustre

Personality is demonstrated with each single move
from grace to tragic ineptitude
but inanimate, history will spar with others

Through my conscious fears and aspirations
I unfold my dreams and passions
though with the failing of light my body will fall derelict

And in a thousand years' time
outlasting it all
in a museum or some lecture hall

the scaffold of my core
may well hang side by side with yours
with labels almost identical

There is no need for the family to huddle round the fire

The focus of the living room is switched to the tv
It sheds a different light
at the touch of a button, at the turn of a dial

instant luke warmth
No-one stares for hours into the heart of a radiator
No-one basks in the glow of underfloor heating

the temperature is maintained uniform throughout
no mess, no inconvenience
like an acquaintance, a lodger, a flat mate

In years to come will Guy Fawkes be sat
on a huge air conditioning unit
whilst we watch fireworks via broadband?

Welcome to the City of Self

The above phrase was found graffiti'd on Edinburgh Art Gallery during the Fringe in 1990

Welcome to the City of Self
where the body of Christ becomes bread and jam
The beast with a thousand I's
I leaflet therefore I am

Winning boat races tie at Oxbridge
careerists frigging in the rigging
It's the death of a sales pitch
where the one line quote is king

Where it takes 200 to tango
Fast talking at the running buffet
Is there a medical student in the house
or is everyone's name really 'lovey'?

Beauty hangs its head
where the commonplace has no worth
where once the touch of another's hand
might have been the greatest show on Earth

There's an old man dead in the gutter
there are razor blades stained by a bath
but in the carnival nothing else matters
except he who gets the last laugh

Tuning up with the 'me me me'
the sell-by-date of the year
If Van Gogh had had to play Edinburgh
he'd have cut off his other ear

Chapel of the Metal Shroud

I stand before you as faith
in accuracy and a system man-made

in distance and the white line
in direction and the painted sign

in measurement and ordained barriers
in technology and the road builders

in evolution and the mechanic's skill
in instinct and the common will

in order over the unknown
in yourself and those close to

in the motives of strangers
in society and human behaviour

Purity of spirit comes in all waist sizes

Patronised as character
the problem is not glandular
The problem is only the perception of glamour
a perfect anatomy provides no real armour

There is no correlation between girth and worth
we play the glands we're dealt at birth
Lift up your chins, live fat die full
build your bonfires on the highest of hills

Physical presence is but a folly
only the depth of the soul is measured as holy
Angels are never spotty, hunchback, nor bald
bone structure is transparent in the weighing of souls

The reflection in the back of God's spoon

Nude modelling for the afterlife
she secures the burger concession in Paradise

It's difficult to be concerned at the world's wrongs
with an industrial base of cream scones

There are dead moths at your alter
Theme parks replacing the landscapes of human nature

There's an empty funhouse with a Formica carousel
A gardener nurturing humanity on the high road to Hell

Originality for the mass market reaped with a vengeance
Individually wrapped tears and brutal indifference

As reproach stalks this poetry in thin disguise
for dogs bound by pavement there is little pride

All the seas of mercy yet to understand
I feel the sadness of computers in an enchanted land

How can the mortician fill dead bodies with formaldehyde
then go home and make love to his wife?

The wasting of limbs and the squandering of belief
Perpetual emotion and the dignity of trees

It's fear of death beating the wings of my heart
I reach for your hand in the dark

I reach for your hand in the dark

Ten ways to end a relationship

After Adrian Mitchell

1. *PATRIOTIC*
   I've got to dedicate myself to work of national importance

2. *SNOBBISH*
   Your time allocation has expired

3. *OVERWEENING*
   You are too fine a human to be held back by constraints

4. *PIOUS*
   I shall pray you find happiness elsewhere

5. *MELODRAMATIC*
   I'll kill myself rather than go through this torture any longer

6. *PATHETIC*
   I'm not worthy of love – I can't stand anyone to see me like this

7. *DEFENSIVE*
   I don't have to give reasons

8. *SINISTER*
   I've been sleepwalking with a bread knife lately

9. *LECHEROUS*
   I want to fuck your best friend

10. *PHILOSOPHICAL*
    Well were we really going out anyway?

There's always room in the hearse on the way back

Joseph plays the percentages
he can be eyeing up four women in different parts of
the same room

He takes his data day diary literally
A wall chart of his sperm level would read like a cardiac arrest
To him love is a dog with six legs

Relationships, just things that crash in the night
Loyalty, a free fall from infatuation to indifference
from the erotic to the erratic

There is a need to prove that he can still compete

To Joseph
nature gives no time to niceties
forever, comes with in-built obsolescence

There always appears a point in coupling when he feels like
he's stuck next to someone on a long coach journey having ran
out of conversation

In despair, it is of course the things we don't say that shout
the loudest
Joseph mutilates his every hour

I don't believe he chooses to be ugly
it is merely an ailment
a sickness of the spirit

Joseph's crime is that of cowardice
He has spent his whole life running with the eye of the storm
and destiny seems such a big word for such a small return

Cranking up suspense in adolescence
the pivot and swerve, the running of the escalator
carnal desire his internationalle
Joseph shies away from the need of a meaning

For the ultimate taboo is to be lonely even for a second
and so to fail, to be an object of pity, to be a loser
and clichés become clichés for a reason
no-one, but no-one, loves a loser

It is to strands of this he ties his final submission

hoping as mortality yawns
hoping as the sediment thaws
hoping as the essence pulls immediate to his breath
that his lies are lies after all

All kids are born with long thin moustaches

Like most kids I suppose I was a natural surrealist
I used to think nothing of playing football for hours
in my cowboy outfit

I had no concept of relative scale
and no distinct understanding of the comparative relationship
between any two objects

My Action Man would regularly hitch lifts
straddled across a 2 inch Matchbox fire engine

Toilet rolls, shoeboxes, Elastoplast reels,
coat hangers and Fairy Liquid bottles
were all stock multi-faceted components
to fit into any imaginary playworld

But never
and I always felt this to be one of the major drawbacks to my creativity
the double-sided sticky tape *Blue Peter* and *Magpie* presenters
somehow always assumed you'd have lying around
For years I pictured all middle class kids having drawers full of the stuff

Large cardboard boxes could change in seconds
from racing cars to jet planes or speed boats
just by a slight alteration in the accompanying engine noise
Any sheet or tablecloth became a tent which I'd just sit in for days
and days and days

One of my very favourite games
was when the British 8th Army desert patrol Airfix soldiers
would fight off the alien spaceship
which was always made out of Lego
and manned by Fuzzy-Felt farm animals

Travelling second class through Hope

With softer spine you rise and shine
and strap yourself safe in time

More beads for the natives, more gongs for the troops
you buy off the kids with spaghetti hoops
melt into the monotone, the drip-feed tv
Death Wish 4, Funland UK, until you say

Is   this   all   there   is   ?

You say you need a cause, you need to fight
you're looking for something, anything
If only you had something noble denied
sometimes you say you'd fight everything

So down at the beast market
you seek solace in your crisps
Hey, what's a nice Jaeger jumper like that
doing in a place like this?

You see Madonna singing 'Material Girl'
to earthquake victims in The Third World

You see a white car drive through Soweto
swords designed as shields
the new credit card diplomacy
and the worship of God on wheels, and you say

Is   this   all   there   is   ?

And when the party's over, and limp lettuce and lager trodden into the
carpet are no longer part of the fun. And you realise that the Earth
doesn't revolve around three pubs in the centre of town. And you realise
your God's not bigger than my God after all. Travelling second class
through Hope, you pray, there must be more than this

Cornerhouse

Permanently at a crossroads
I glory in my window seat
The goldfish outside
don't realise the irony of the screenplay for
today I am Richard Baseheart
Schools of buses
migrate towards Piccadilly Gardens
as I chart a course for the rest of my life
People with bigger fish to fry
circle the glass
their faces mouthing in silence

Yesterday I was mistaken for Bergman
in Panoramic Cinemascope
austere against a backdrop of grey and white
but no... I was on top of a bus
front seat
bound for Skegness

Then 2000 years later that afternoon
on the bridge of the Enterprise
I was left in control of the console
the red alert button
resembling a buttered scone
screen on
Spock dead
my ship infested with aliens
my finger poised over a protruding sultana

But today
my body feels as heavy as a shipwreck
I am safe in the deep of my third cuppa
periscope down
listening for sonar
avoiding the sharks and the mermaids

1. ...for want of a better word we call it love

With your leg bent over mine I can feel the moistness of your desire
With your breast cupped against my lifeline I can feel the flourish
    of your heart
There is a dance within your pulse

2. Some days I lie in bed all morning waiting for the phone to ring

I could get up but I need outside intervention
some stimulus, catalyst, impetus
the doorbell to buzz, the landlord to knock,
the window cleaner to bruise his ladders against the paintwork
a poster to fall from the wall, the bedroom to burst into flames
anything

I am already dead
my carcass exhumed to imitate devotion
Some days I close my eyes
and take my heart off the hook

3. Though the world now lies empty as the dialogue in a cheap
    porn movie

once, maybe
on another continent
where the sky seemed wider
allowing arms to stretch out and loosen the joints

If there is no such thing as true love then all logic is built
on the smallest unit of time

Only Christmas and birthdays bring death this close

Overnight you have grown old
and though spite is no spur to succeed
in the absence of caress it can suffice

Only yesterday
with hair dye and vitamins
you boasted you had cheated time
but now it is the last dance of the party and
the prospect of a taxi home alone
rises like a flush within your cheeks

Years you wasted
slip through the doorway
giggling together adolescent
clear skin and eyes so bright
and always with partners that look such fools
but young

It is not them you hate but their youth
There is no individuality in this attraction merely the
aesthetics of innocence
and you, clinging to that one chance
force yourself into the night air before
the indignity of being the last to leave

I have seen you in the morning
lost in some mundane task
unaware of my presence
There is a subtlety of emotion that wisps around your eyes
You hesitate behind each door
What worries you most is the loss of appetite

Where once you were so sure
diplomatic farewells have beaten back your pride
Where once you were curious
the nakedness of longing has sought to scar your faith
breathe still
no whim of nature will chill your soul tonight

there are traditions that carry the truth of seasons
there are books that will outlast technology
we are old friends you and I
rest your fears against these words
it'll be alright
it will be alright

The 44th minute

All I want now is
to be in wonder
immersed

Reminded purity exists
somewhere
in this universe

New friends tell me I've become disfigured in repartee

that all softness or aggression is passé
that detachment is sophistication
To think it should come to this
Her eyes were emerald
and there was a simple joy
in watching her brush her hair

As if bewitched by childhood I have seen you dazzle
I have lightened my frown to the bond of sweethearts
I have chanced the whirlwind of derision
and as enchantment ends
on yet another carriage I cower from
Chinese whispers that taunt floodlights on my illusions

Sometimes I wonder if I've ever been in love
it's like trying to explain why a joke is funny

No matter how I feign indifference I still fear flying
As each plane leaves the ground my prayers are of you
If the soul survives I want above all to hold your presence
This may not weigh heavy in the glib torrent of conversation
but at times such as these those moribund do not lie
not to themselves

I realise to you I am already fable
It seems I lost you even before we met
Don't look at me now
I've grown old and ugly
whilst you remain
breathless as a new constellation

February

Least favoured of the dozen

She does not promote sales like January
to some the first disappointment of the calendar

She does not offer optimism or resolve with the
freshness of a truly clean sheet

She does not promise new life
with the same authority as her replacement

She is never sure how she should be clothed
the best winter costumes already modelled

The spring collection held back
there is a feeling of making up the numbers

February is a corridor of a month
Leap year she smiles that extra smile

but it is the fleeting smile of a receptionist
or a cloakroom attendant

She licked the applause from the fingers of each hand
like honey drips from toast
but could never hold on tight enough
to that for which she hungered most

Only let into the heart like a holiday home
though always a paying guest
Scratching for dignity from blind hope
but knowing dignity is still second best

Love has always been one of those rooms at parties
that she'd never dare venture inside
where close friends sat cross-legged on floorboards
and she had no invite

Always outstretched arms at railway stations
into which she'd never run
or couples on buses in matching jumpers
unashamed to dress as one

This time though she thought she'd sneaked unnoticed
into the gates of Heaven accepted for her sins
but she clung too tight never understanding
how fragile a thing are wings

and when the regret welled up inside
there was no cradle for her soul and her broken pride
How can it hurt so much if the love has died?

and soon all the narrow eyes and shallow lives
became a noose around her neck
until accelerating into fog the drink cocooned her head
how can you love so much and have nothing left?

Within your arms

If you were
      water
I would laze in your caress
and if you were fire
I would bathe in your passion

If you were air
I would breathe in your perfume
and if
    you were wool
I would wrap myself in your warmth

and
if you were
      darkness
I would lose myself in you
        forever

Why you never look like Paul Newman on family photos

Snapshots snag real life
full of misdirected angles

blurred vision
faces disappearing off edges

people betrayed by their expression
likenesses half caught

shadows masking the image
outlines cluttered and confused

poses thrown by the unexpected
objects obstructing the foreground

strangers intruding into the background
characters unready or self conscious

identities distorted by perspective
detail erased by exposure

features too close to register but more often too far away
figures dwarfed by a vast expanse of sky

The third person

Using they instead of I
they generalize
and rationalise to anaesthetise

from the emote to the remote
in the they and the he
in the they and the she

They no longer enjoy they appreciate
They no longer experience they spectate

bureaucrats of passion
they no longer feel but relate
they no longer talk but discuss
they no longer argue but debate
they no longer react but equate

They dilute to nullify
from the nib to the cursor
as they distance themselves
in the third person

Dopey and Juliet

We are watching a new adaptation of *Romeo and Juliet* but
it is ridiculous to empathise with the leading characters

Mawkish fascination has laid waste to my valour
and my body creaks like a faulty windscreen wiper

I can no longer read the nakedness of your face
How I react is no reflection on you
How you react is not necessarily a reflection on me

Your eyes remain unchanged but
you wear the years apart like a new fashion

I'm sure the main actors mock my tentative appearance in this scene
I would feel easier if this were *Beauty and the Beast*
or more comfortable even with the part of Dopey in *Snow White*

You touch my hand and reassure me that we can be friends now
I'm certain in your version I'm not even in this play

I have taken on the role of an old work colleague that it's
nice to see for two minutes but could become tiresome over the
course of a few drinks

❧

Your elbow is close but you can't bite it

Now smarts like laughter in the art gallery
like the piercing of a balloon
like the panic mid-fall

A revelation too commonplace
any bride's father
awaiting the wedding car could explain

The past – some other lifetime away
paling intuition
growing on the back of now

The future – a scaffold to infinity
possible now to be relished
promises of now in which to excel

A conscious now holds my hand
deliberate amid a most solid universe
now so loud Cupid would need ear defenders

I am sitting with you again

As usual you are courting solitude
You are browsing possible lifestyles
and though I am troubled by the vivid contrast
I will not discolour this silence

Lost within your glossy magazine
colour co-ordinated rooms do not allow
for the frailty of the hesitant
and the self-conscious

I will try to fake nonchalance when your eyes eventually
look up from the page
In the time it takes
for a breath to change from inward to outward
we are re-writing a new future

I am sitting with you again
You are somewhere
where the stars offer different possibilities
but there is no distance between us

Civic statues are never naked

Proud for posterity
Jaw set
Self-aware
Inactive
Like a solid photograph
This is the official face
Formal dress
Dignity without vulnerability
A permanent Sunday best
Grandeur selected to inspire
Without tenderness
Sterner than life
Humanity reduced
for the importance of stonework

Hypnotized by oncoming headlights
the idiot beguiled
with humour as bleak as a highland loch
mocked with accommodating smiles

Still looking for love as hardy as bluebells
betrayal's quite funny really
we hide emotions behind glass
never seeing too clearly

Infatuation's a sight common enough
a love-lost caricature
just another walk on part
with delusions of grandeur
who would kiss your blood
and believe it pure

Eternal promises are for All Fools Day
comically cruel
so mist now softens the skyline
whilst I band aid the ridicule

In the open court of mountains like 12 angry jurors
I serve my solitude
I feel no guilt, though I know I shouldn't
I miss you

Time passed unnoticed until she took the clock

Slumped on your chair like dead weight at an orgy
coughing like an S-reg Fiat
though you've lit up a thousand churches in prayer
you know she's not coming back

Overfat on time,
you say 'age doesn't matter' then you lie about your own
if you live to be 100 you'd still be afraid of dying too young
switching off the bedside lamp shadows crowd the void
but the patterns on the wallpaper don't scare you anymore
it's the blank spaces now that threaten
Nothing, not even love, survives within a vacuum

Fast approaching your love-by date
you count the days left unkissed
Age
has become just another stick to beat yourself with

Where once your passion was an elevator between Heaven and Hell
Where once you believed love dripped from between her legs

There in the absence of children
sex grew tired on easy living
becoming a parasite on the back of routine
and all the words you chose so carefully
blew like so much litter
Conversations became quieter
and as scarce as in a spaghetti western
Laughter became a missing person

until
you couldn't remember kissing her face when you last made love

and her lips became just hooks to hang your heart upon
and though you look for that face from the window of every train
the photo in your pocket is now starting to fade
and though you curse the new diary with each year that arrives
you never noticed the clock on the wall until it kissed you goodbye
you never noticed the clock on the wall until it kissed you goodbye

Learning to understand the mechanics of the eclipse

Only the youngest of women left their scent
and friends thought this an inadequacy
Whilst to Nick, as he would have you believe
it was between himself and God alone

Licking the thighs of other women
in the naked sighs of other women
Nick blurred into all humanity

In the schedules of other women he sipped tea
In the flurry of sweat and breath he fought to contain the clouds
Whether he tripped, or was pushed, or whether he jumped
he glimpsed weakness, once and forever weakness

Pressed to the nipple of other women
he crowded his floors
with the tissue bodies of liquid promises
and the scattered mourning clothes of bloodrush and desire

Until, between the devil and the deep blue eyes
grief like a panther fell on him
but here now curled up in his arms
the crying wound of another's penance

Nick had become a bit player in another's nostalgia
Between empty sheets
token gifts winced at the coldness of dead flesh
Here, the softest of mirrors

and now, time to discover
just how pure the bottom line
just how myopic the personification of love
just how selfish melancholy

The accidental death of a cat

Outside the polling office
I saw a cat that had never voted
run over by a man-made machine
that failed to notice

Like a circus crowd
a random cross-section of the electorate
spectated, as spasms of pain
jerked the body into acrobatics

Someone went to phone
but to phone who?
Someone went to find the owner
Someone went for a half brick

the cat lay still at last, one eye dangling loose
like a battered old teddy bear
The half brick was discarded
The cat placed reverently into a Safeway's carrier bag

The crowd dispersed
The afternoon sun dried
the small smudges of blood
into the tarmac

The colours meshed so that soon you
could hardly notice the difference
when you passed
Later than night all parties claimed victory

No game show will ever hold your worth

I noticed on your windowsill
two broken flowers in a small glass
These were not set in pride of place but lay unassuming
like children huddled in the dark

Their stems too short now to fit the vase
convenience would have them dumped in a bin liner
but something in you
could not let even this
seemingly dispensable
frail beauty die

I know such an action is no great gesture but only a tiny
moment in a far corner of the rush
but it is a victory
an everyday victory
and its colour should flutter within each heart

You, who are capable of such casual tenderness
what worlds your palms could describe
no game show will ever hold your worth
no computer ever measure your soul

whilst there is the merest glimmer of humanity
we are none of us lost

we are not lost

A farce is still a farce even with subtitles

and she tells me she loves him
with her hand stroking my inner thigh
Her face is symmetrical and her sweat has a pleasant composition
We are exchanging pretty lies like cigarette cards

Stifling disinterest like two old soldiers between battles
The mutual gratification of animal lust seems a distinct possibility
We are both whores to romance
but it is all too predictable

There is no pilgrimage in her fingertips
only the musing of calculation
and I wonder if my face displays its weariness
An idle stubble scratches the sheen from her make up

There is no nourishment in these overtures
only the mechanics of anatomy, a series of shrugs
How can your blood race so fast
but your heart remain unmoved

I don't have to wait for the morning to hate myself
Pitiful and pathetic seem insults too well used to scald disgust

When I look into the mirror, if I concentrate on the centre
features of my face, I can see how I used to look in my teens
Is it guilt that's swollen my neck
or my face wrapping itself against the world?

The desire to wipe the slate clean, to start a new jotter
competes each day against the easier option to drown all vivid
images in maudlin and lie, before God's feet, face down in the
subway, stained with my own piss

As you can see I try my best to romanticise this predicament
but tacky affairs always remind me of cheap early seventies movies

I turn my back when we've made love

I turn my back when we've made love
but not turned against you
My thoughts are of you
the curve of your body marks the horizon
the scent of you I cherish along my skin
Memories of our sex perfumes distant vales
blood has not yet settled

I've slept this way since childhood
through marriage and a dozen affairs
Unfortunately there are some things you can't un-learn
In sleep as in spirit we fall alone
though I long to drift in endless embrace
though open mouthed I wish for the cliché of souls entwined
this is the folly of gift shops

I will always sleep apart
Lie close
and still
we are tired as only lovers can be

Love – the disaster movie

she said she hated you / loathed you / found you utterly repulsive / but you tried not to take it personally / now you're standing in an empty room making a cup of tea you don't want / and being over-nice to people you hate / measuring your success by counting the things you'll never have / you turn on the tv to watch black and white nothing / for a few pounds more you could have coloured nothing / you go to the pessimists' club twice a week now, it gives you something to look forward to / you used to worry about your lack of troubles / lying in the sun praying you didn't get skin cancer / now you're trying to capture the world in one sentence / dressed as lamb, you beef about the price of love / dressed to kill you sacrifice yourself / standing in your perfect world you look out of place / oh the words you almost said may make you great someday / if only you knew the rules you'd ignore them / you shrug your shoulders, some you lose... and some you lose / there's plenty more fish in the sea you said, but now diving in you feel like a fish out of water and look for corners in the goldfish bowl / people tell you to be yourself but that's not like you / when you're not thinking of her / you're thinking of thinking of her / you see yourself as a prisoner trapped in a world of reason / whose crime is that of wanting her / whose sentence is that of loving her / and whose only escape is to her / you're living in a world of aliens / you feel like the skeleton in your own cupboard / like someone's playing loud music at your funeral / it's no fun being depressed you complain / with the ultimate vanity you believe your inferiority complex is of a superior nature / you believe some people wouldn't recognise love if you beat them to a pulp with it / what did she mean we've got nothing in common? you say / it's her, I've got plenty in common / you wonder whether you'd rather be loved / or love someone / or be in love with someone you love and who loves you / and realise you don't ask for much / you used to be lovers / now you're just good friends / that means she ignores you as though an embarrassment / and you watch your words when you meet unexpectedly / I used to be sensitive you explain / but I'm alright now, do you think?

Someone tossed a match into the corner of our past

Someone tossed a match into a corner of our past
It was the darkest corner
where rubbish had collected unseen

Out of curiosity
I kindled the flame.
By its flicker I could gradually recognise
each item of debris

Sickened with fascination
I nurtured the fervour until it blazed with fury
casting shadows onto the rest of our lives

It raged with self-destruction.
It raged with despair
Everything and anything it could
it would drag down and wound

Until
wounded itself, blind and dying
strangled by its own appetite
it shrunk and curled

I leave the ashes now as a reminder
I ought really to clear them away
They seem so small reduced to cinder

It's childish I know but
the heat has scorched so much
I have to show you before they're
finally swept

Demoting Cupid to a chat show host

I'm having to be polite
with someone whose nipples I licked
less than seven days since
Someone whose craving
hung so vulnerable on my fingertips

It's a strange courage
that sees flight as dignity
She is talking to me now in the language of social workers
offering fragments of explanation
like corners from some complicated jigsaw

Waving at the window
as if to wipe an image from the glass
When a child falls
there's a moment when
it doesn't know whether to laugh or cry

It seems at the narrowest junctions
my future sits before me
purposely waiting for the lights to change
then indicates
against the oncoming traffic

Hell is a place where all the photos you thought you'd safely destroyed are enlarged

Yesterday
all the litter that I'd thrown away throughout my life
came round to visit me

It demanded to be let in
said we needed to talk

Feeling guilty at the ease with which I'd so conveniently discarded it
I let it in
There hardly seemed room for it all

The used tea bags alone filled the kitchen
and there were margarine tubs and toenail clippings
I hadn't seen for ten years or more

Strange now to think
how they used to be very much part of my life at one time
I confess I found it difficult to relate

I've changed a lot
I'm sure some of the litter has changed
It's bound to have
The half used tin of tomatoes from April 1964 certainly had

A chipped mug with no handle took the initiative
it asked why I never rang
'I kept meaning to,' I lied, 'but I've lost the number'

The number itself
cowered on a screwed up piece of paper and said nothing

Sharing the same piece of paper
the words 'I'm sure we can still be good friends'
blushed like felt tip.

Several old shoes, a left handed glove,
a recent batch of razor blades and numerous bread wrappers
each with one crust left in
began to edge round the topic of coming back

The remains of an Airwick Solid opened up trying
to clear the air

The atmosphere was getting a little uncomfortable
A few old fly papers conceded
that they had never really held out much hope
and had only come along with the rest

There was an awkward silence
when I introduced the new bin bags

Eventually I managed to persuade
all but one or two piccalilli jars
that coming back maybe wasn't such a good idea

and after a few hours
we parted amicably enough

I don't think there'll be any further visits
for a while at least

even so
I don't know that I like the way
the swing bin now looks at me
knowingly

King Street

I once set myself adrift at a jumble sale
watching pregnant craving in frenzy

And I have no wish to pretend I am in London
I have no desire to be at the centre of things

When I couldn't afford to buy
these windows intimidated

Today they are like Christmas trimmings
left up too long

Once I turn the corner onto Cross Street
I am back in Manchester

The ratio of stone to glass
suggesting a reflection of substance

Mixed metaphors

Upon recognition, an outburst of enthusiasm and then
we'd probably struggle to find something in common

Old friends seeking points of reference
as awkward as mixed metaphors

with words like anticlimax and disappointment lurking in the wings
but even so, I'd still like us to meet up again someday

ideally in passing, when rushing for a train
with just enough time to test the water

sketch in the bare bones of a future conversation
and most importantly, in case we never meet again

to say those simple but difficult things we should, but never do, say
consoling ourselves with phrases like 'can't be put into words'

Those most important of things never said but
just drowned in the moment and lost in the shuffle

Tomorrow's worms (a love poem to critics)

Born
without
backbones
they ooze
from their
holes
they are
processors
of sewage
a linear
arse machine
two faced
they digest
and excrete
they're
proof
you are
what you eat
a cannibal
realisation
of reincar-
nation
experts
deem them
necessary
for more
than just
easy quarry
bad weather
brings them
to the
surface
if you
cut them
in two
do it
length
ways

Recoiling from the anticlimax

I have seen disappointment
in eyes like undertakers
sizing up my future

in limp handshakes
and blank glances at wristwatches
in the tactical retreat to the toilet

in forced smiles
and edgy non-specific answers
in the shifting of focus

in conversations that talk around or over
sometimes even through
in the contortions of cocktail diplomacy

in the appointment remembered
in the sudden relapse
in the unexpected duty

in the body language of the dispassionate
in those with the ease to mingle
and as always

I am left with the awkwardness
knowing that any gesture I make
any fight any sacrifice

will be
a disappointment

Owning imperfection

We are the imperfect
the rejected
the bruised
the damaged goods
the misshapen fruit

the crop that failed to make the grade
the eggshell that couldn't take the strain
the discounted
the allowable waste
the below standard

the bottom of the range
the potatoes with too many eyes
the slow mover putrefied
the garment soiled
the bargain spoiled

the chipped and cracked
the squeezed and put back
the peas no longer tender and young
the incomplete
the thread undone

the scorned
the squashed
the marked
down
the grape unwashed

We are the imperfect
the rejected
the bruised
the aborted
the discontinued

Silence of the phone

The silence of the phone
is not just the silence of one person
but the silence of all humanity

Not only does she not want to speak to you
nobody wants to speak to you
not one person in the entire world

You are not only alone
but snubbed, ignored
rebuked by a conspired silence

A deliberate vindictive silence
not a pause or a shared silence
but a cold desolate silence

A silence
for which you are responsible
Your silence

There are many silences
the silence that passes between lovers unnoticed
the silence of a baby's sleep

the silence of a couple trapped in indifference
the silence of an empty chair
the silence before a suicide

and the silence of the phone
is the sum of all these
and more

When the time has come to leave

You can always tell when the time has come to leave
your things start to get put away in cupboards and drawers
out of sight

conversations quieten
people are busy when you enter a room
nobody looks you in the face or asks how you are

Mime doesn't pay

Last night I was burgled by a mime artist
He never made a sound

He could have got away with it
but then he tried to steal a piano I haven't got

He pushed and he pulled, he strained and he heaved
but it wouldn't move

Maybe, he thought, there was something valuable behind it
There wasn't

He tried to float the piano

He blew up a balloon and tied it to the piano
then he couldn't lift the balloon

I found him in the morning trapped inside an imaginary box

I called the police
He started to panic
tried climbing up a fictitious ladder

When the police arrived they let him out
He made a dash for it
tried running away on the spot.

It took the police four hours to get him into the car
he kept getting pulled back by an invisible rope

I decided not to press charges
This afternoon I put an insurance claim in for the piano

Your favourite mug

Foolish I know
but I feel protective towards your favourite mug
I leave it around the house

as though you were still between sips
as if your lips were just out of the room a moment
and would soon enter and caress its brim

Alone at bedtime
I hold it gently, feel its warmth
and drink you in once more

Breaking up is...

Breaking up is...
making a conscious effort to say 'I' instead of 'we'
taking your number down from beside the phone

trying to play only records you never liked
pretending to be busy
trying to think of people worse off

mutual friends being diplomatic
saying 'at least you're both still young'
and 'at least you've got your health'

and other sentences all starting with 'at least'
planning the weekend around half a dozen eggs

not knowing what to do with hands
when walking down the street
finding people who look like you attractive

forgiving you everything
then nothing every other minute
discounting years in seconds

wanting to talk
but wishing too much hadn't been said already

Beyond mathematics

How much do I love thee?
Let me calculate the ways

Take the number of kisses
on the bottom of my letters
times
by the phone calls on your answering machine

Then add
warm bodies on winter nights
holding hands along the beach
and the moment you first thought of

Divide by
the forgotten anniversaries
the turning of a key in silence
and the emptiness of a meal for one

And what are you left with?

She has given herself

She has given herself
to the majesty of clouds discoloured
and the face of the moon dying in the west

She has given herself to the seasons
to the dreams of childhood
and to that which she can heal with her own hands

She has given herself to the storm from open sea
to the silence of a cold bed
and to the flight of the highest wing across the glare

If by chance she should see God
she would stare him full in the face
and would never be the first to look away

I'm talking to someone else's father

I was
I suppose
gay around the age of twelve and thirteen

Though to be honest
glandular activity being what it is
nothing was safe around that time

I'd have attempted sexual intercourse
with a tin of Swarfega
if that was the only way of achieving orgasm

It is quite common for lads
to become sexually aroused
climbing over furniture

It is not considered incitement
in these later years
to offer me a chair when I visit

When your eyes say 'I am here – is that not enough?'

James reaches out to grasp at something tangible
He counts the number of words in your compliment

He sets every affection into an overall picture
measures every gift against the past

If you tell him you love him he'll note it down
and consider it later

If you like a particular song he'll examine the words
for telltale signs of subconscious infidelity

If you cry he'll wonder if you're crying
for something he can't give you

In the happiest moments he steps back
and looks for approval

Even with eyes caught in a tender exchange
he feels lonely

He fears one morning when nothing in particular
seems to have happened
you'll come to him with your goodbye neatly folded
Even now your words haunt his pillow
Even now your words haunt his pillow

Happiness

Happiness
   is relative
    a   distant   relative
the sort you see once a year
 and can never stop long

The lost generation of mermen and mermaids

I've flushed most of my descendants down the loo
unconsummated angels on clouds of tissue

I have squandered over five billion emissaries
en route to fertile ovaries

Wasted another five million destination unknown
stunting their growth much more than my own

Whole cemeteries of condoms I've created
non starters not begat but now belated

The dumped diehard deliverers of DNA
trashed tadpole triggers of the family way

Minute Duncan Goodhews that got no further
than gossamer graves and milky mass murder

Cul-de-sac germination
timely entrapment and termination

A self-induced final solution
ethnic cleansing of my own evolution

Plain biscuits

Why do rich people insist it's
posh to eat plain biscuits

It seems to me Rich Tea are for the miserly
and Nice are not nice at any price
Shortbread I particularly dread
I'd sooner have a Happy Face instead

Tradition is fine for old codgers
but the young at heart want Jammy Dodgers
A plain Digestive is strictly for the restive
and not suggestive of anything festive

Similarly Garibaldis
are for the oldies
as only old fogies can be force-fed
a sandwich of bogies

Morning Coffee are easy to debunk
being impossible to dunk
An Arrowroot bicky
can also be tricky

Abbey Crunch or Bourbon Creams
are not the munch of my dreams
I'd sooner walk on hot coals bare foot
than eat Fig Rolls or Ginger Nut

and I'd sooner be aborted
than touch Teatime Assorted

yet I can eat Chocolate Hobnobs
no probs

A happy ending (revised)

...and they all lived happily ever after.

Well not all. Not all the time that is.

You've got to remember the book may have taken four or five hours to read but its story was meant to span several years. They obviously picked out the main action and discarded the mundane. You know, the trips to the toilet, the coming back to close the curtains, the days when someone wasn't feeling very clever so they just took it easy... that sort of stuff.

So when it says 'they all lived happily ever after' you have to take it as read there'd still be days, even weeks when nothing much happened. Someone might get a bit bored or feel a bit so so about an idea. Someone else might feel tired all of a sudden or feel that life was becoming repetitive, or passing them by.

The film was only an hour fifteen which meant they missed out a lot of the book. They even spiced up a few scenes to enhance the action.

So when it says 'they all lived happily ever after'
they meant that, on the whole, given the human condition
they had a relatively happy existence
remembering that they'd got over the worst of the bad stuff
during the making of the story,
forming as it did the basis of the plot
and given that we left the main characters on a high
as is the nature of romanticised story telling leading to such
an obviously flawed generalisation.

To Helena and back

There is no reasoning to your loneliness
You build your fireside on the most barren of landscapes
You offer your resignation from the vital

You are too concerned with structure and process

Those that wallow in reminiscence
suffocating all bitterness in nostalgia
deny the pain that the body needs
to summon the adrenaline
to heal the wound

But such observation is cerebral
even the sound of the vowels is the betrayal of compassion
It's actions not words that provide the most vivid memory

The gift I would bring to your christening
is courage in all things

Let the optimism you wear shame all contrived fashion

Unholy in the church of perfection
the stairs to forgiveness
are worn with the footsteps of those that falter

And you hold up your arms to the world
You wear desperation like a weight around your shoulders

There is no reason why I should save you

There is no reason why you should save me

I have this theory that when you die your whole life is re-run like a sensorama video and you have to sit through it all again, every second, unedited, in a room with every friend and every relative that's been in the least bit involved. Now depending on what sort of life you've led this could be Heaven or it could be Hell. Think about it, everyone's going to see those private moments, those very private moments: farting in the bath; wiping bogies down the side of the armchair; every second of indulgent masturbation.

All the pathetic lies you told exposed for all to see; all the naff chat-up lines you used when you were a teenager, and still used later; all the places you had sex when you still lived at home. The things you did to get by; the way you justified it all to yourself and every really dumb-arsed no-balls shit-for-brains mistake you ever made you'll have to watch yourself make again.

But then
     maybe
          there'll be those moments of rare beauty; the moments of tenderness; the times you cried because you messed up; the things you meant to say; the questions in the mirror; the promises you made when you first held your own child; the nights you comforted another's despair; the time your lover's face glowed like beauty on fire; the times you said 'I love you' and believed your love would outlive the universe. The time you first held in your stomach thinking no-one would notice, and the regret in your eyes when you feared you were getting old. When you couldn't sleep one night and lay awake sweating and praying you didn't die before doing something, something, just something.